Leabharlainn nan Eilean Siar

KT-383-419

698.232

99300653J

SCHOOL
LIBRARY
STOCK

WITHDRAWN

10·99

LAND OF THE LONG WHITE CLOUD

KIRI TE KANAWA

LAND OF THE LONG WHITE CLOUD

Maori Myths, Tales and Legends

❖ ILLUSTRATED BY MICHAEL FOREMAN ❖

WESTERN ISLES
LIBRARIES
993 00653J

J398.232

PAVILION
MICHAEL JOSEPH

First published in Great Britain in 1989 by
PAVILION BOOKS LIMITED
196 Shaftesbury Avenue, London WC2H 8JL
in association with Michael Joseph Limited
27 Wrights Lane, Kensington, W8 5TZ

Text copyright © Kiri Te Kanawa 1989
Illustrations copyright © Michael Foreman 1989

Edited by Anne Gatti

Designed by Janet James

All rights reserved. No part of this publication
may be reproduced, stored in a retrieval system, or
transmitted, in any form or by any means, electronic,
mechanical, photocopying, recording or otherwise,
without the prior permission of the copyright holder.

A CIP catalogue record for this book is
available from the British Library
ISBN 1 85145 176 5

Printed and bound in Singapore
by Toppan Printing Company

10 9 8 7 6 5 4 3 2

Contents

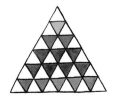

Dedicated to the memory of my mother and father,
Tom and Nell Te Kanawa

Preface

I was lucky enough to have been born and brought up in the beautiful Land of the Long White Cloud, New Zealand. My father was Maori but my mother was a Pakeha, a white person.

New Zealand was a wonderful country to grow up in, and I had a very happy childhood surrounded by many Maori friends and relations. Some of my very best memories of childhood are of being told magical bedtime stories by my mother, who had a special gift for story-telling, and listening, wide-eyed, with other children while one of my many cousins, aunts or uncles related the stories of why and how so many of the places where we played had come to be given their special names.

New Zealand is a country of green fields, lakes and rivers, all gloriously beautiful, and one really has to visit to appreciate what they look like. My friends and I, of course, loved to play outdoors. One of my favourite places was Lake Taupo where I used to love to go fishing and sailing with my father. I love the many Maori stories of fishing and boating adventures because they remind me of those wonderful expeditions. The most special time of all was spent with my father, sleeping under the stars on the edge of the lake so that we could be first up to catch the early trout.

My work now takes me all over the world and far away from my homeland. Sadly, I have not lived there for many years. However, I do try to get back to New Zealand as often as I can.

Late in 1987 there was an enormous gathering of all the Te Kanawas at our ancestral home in Te Kuiti. My father was brought up there and the Te Kanawa's own marae, our meeting ground, is situated on a hill outside of town.

The wonderful celebrations lasted for three days with feasting, dancing and singing. Over two hundred of my family joined in and most slept on the floor of the meeting house in sleeping bags. It was an unforgettable reunion of the Te Kanawa clan.

For me, it was particularly nostalgic. In that warm atmosphere, as we swapped stories and caught up on news of so many old friends, powerful memories of my childhood came flooding back and old familiar stories came to mind. I suddenly felt an urge to put pen to paper to share some of those stories that meant so much to me.

By a stroke of luck the illustrator, Michael Foreman, was in New Zealand at the same time and was with us for part of the festivities. He met my family, enjoyed Maori hospitality and in this way had a rather special introduction to Maori culture and the Maori love of story-telling. I was thrilled that he was there and therefore able to translate something of the atmosphere of that occasion through his unique illustrations.

The stories in this book are purely my recollection of those tales that I remembered and loved best when I was a child. Like all good stories they have probably changed in the telling and I am sure there are as many versions of the tales as there are tellers. To refresh my memory I carried out limited research but I made no attempt to 'authenticate' the stories – I simply wanted to record them as I remembered them and thus share my own childhood enjoyment.

I hope they will give you a glimpse of the unique Maori culture that so coloured my childhood and that one day you may have the chance to visit some of the places mentioned in these stories – places like Taupo, Te Kuiti or Rotorua – but watch out for the talking taniwha!

Kiri Te Kanawa

The Birth
of Maui

This is the story of the birth of Maui who grew up to be a maker of mischief and a trickster. He was the fifth and youngest son of Taranga and was known as Maui-tikitiki-a-Taranga, Maui-born-in-the-topknot-of-Taranga. This tale explains why.

Out in the middle of the wide, wide ocean, where the sky rests on the edges and there is no land to be seen, a little bundle of seaweed rose and fell in the swell. Seabirds wheeled around overhead, their lonely cries echoing across the water. The sun beat down and a breeze stirred the surface, pushing the seaweed for miles and miles.

Eventually the bundle drifted in sight of a large piece of land and here the sea delivered it, still intact, onto a sandy shore. The seaweed had become tangled with jellyfish and clouds of flies soon settled on it as the birds continued to circle overhead. A cold wind blew up across the exposed beach.

As luck would have it, this stretch of beach was overlooked by a house on the clifftop, and the house belonged to Tama, a powerful sea god. Now Tama could see a heap of seaweed and jellyfish washed up on the land, and the birds circling above it, but he took no notice of it at first.

A little while later he thought he heard the cry of a baby so he decided to go down to the water's edge to see for himself. He climbed down the steep path to the shore but all he could see was the pile of seaweed and the birds. The crying seemed to be coming from the seaweed so he walked over to it. He bent down, pulled the jellyfish away, and there, wrapped in a coil of human hair, lay a tiny boy baby.

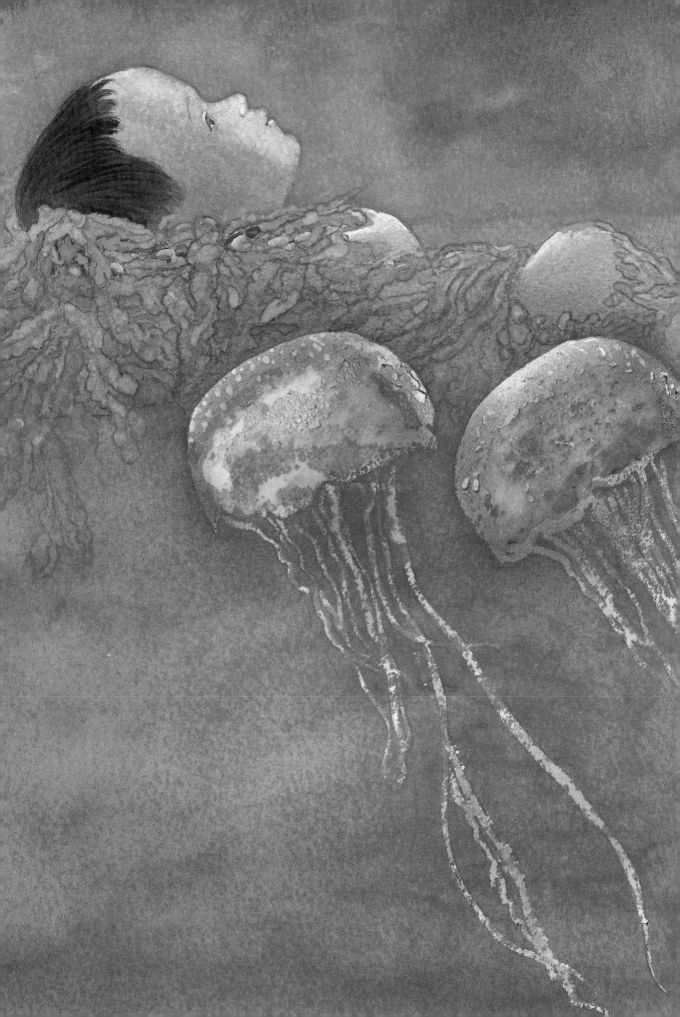

Tama quickly picked up the cold bundle and rushed back up the path towards his house. There he washed the salt water off the baby, wrapped him in a feather cloak and hung him in the rafters above the warmth of the fire.

Now Tama recognized that this tiny baby was Maui, the demi-god, and he was very relieved to have saved his life. While Maui slept Tama found a way of crushing food and softening it so that Maui could eat it. Gradually Maui gained strength and as he grew Tama found that he was delighted to have the company of another human being, even though caring for the baby meant that he no longer had time to sit and look out over the sea, as he used to do.

Tama loved the little boy. When Maui was able to walk and talk he would run out and look at the beautiful clear sky and the sun, and the birds would fly down and flock around him, and they seemed to understand what he was saying to them. As he grew older, Maui knew the names and habits of all the birds, of the sea and the forest, and he called them his lifelong friends.

'Be careful,' warned Tama, 'because they won't always be your friends.'

At times Tama would talk to him in riddles, like this. But he also taught him how fishes lived and spoke to each other, how other people lived – how they grew kumaras in the garden to feed their tribes, how they hunted for birds and fishes, and how they danced and sang in their meeting houses.

Tama played games with Maui too, and told him exciting stories about battles and raids. And when the day was over and they were sitting in the firelight in Tama's house, Tama would teach Maui certain magic tricks, tricks that Maui would use later, to the amazement of his brothers.

When Maui was nearly fully grown Tama grew sad. He knew that Maui would soon have to go out and find his people. But Maui said,

'We will always be friends, Tama, won't we? You are like a father to me.'

And Tama was proud of him and said, 'Maui, you have been a great student. I will love you always.'

Another winter passed and Tama called to Maui one day and said,

'I must send you away now. I have been like a father and a mother to you but now I feel that my bones are old and that I must soon set off for the Underworld and see my old friends.'

So Maui said farewell to Tama over many nights and thanked him for being a father and a mother to him. Then he gathered his clothes, took food for several days, and set off on his journey.

He walked many miles through forests, around lakes and up mountains. He passed many a village and saw many groups of people. But he kept on going until, at last, he came to one particular village. He walked right into it and entered the very first house he saw. As soon as he stepped inside he had a powerful feeling of belonging. He knew that he had found his family.

Maui saw four tall young men and a beautiful woman who was talking to the men.

'Now, my young sons,' she was saying, 'come with me. We will all be dancing tonight in the meeting house and I want to make sure that you're ready.'

Maui crept in behind the last one as the tallest of them stepped forwards.

'I am here, Mother.'

'Oh, there you are, Maui-mua Maui-the-first,' she said, and as the others followed suit she counted them. 'Maui-roto Maui-the-middle, that's two. Maui-taha Maui-the-side, that's three. And Maui-pae Maui-the-edge, that's four. Now we're all ready.'

Just then Maui stood out of the shadows and spoke up,

'I am Maui too.'

Baffled at the sight of this stranger, the mother stared hard and then replied, 'No, I have my four sons. I have counted them.'

But Maui insisted that he was Maui too, and the mother came close to him with a lighted stick and said,

'Let me look at you. I have never seen you before. You are a stranger. Who are you really?'

And he said,

'I am Maui, little Maui, and I am no stranger. I am your son.'

'But I have no other sons,' she replied.

'Are you sure?' asked Maui.

The mother stood silently for a few moments and then spoke, hesitatingly.

'Well . . . there was a little baby . . . but he died . . . and I wrapped him in my hair and the wind took him away . . .' She paused and then asked Maui, almost in a whisper, 'What is my name?'

'Your name is Taranga.'

Her eyes widened with surprise and filled with tears. Then she stepped forwards and embraced him, saying,

'Yes, you are Maui, my little Maui. I shall call you Maui-tikitiki-a-Taranga, Maui-formed-in-the-topknot-of-Taranga.'

And so it was that Maui came to live with his mother and his four brothers and that his mother delighted in the return of her last-born son.

Maui and the
Great Fish

This is the story of how Maui caught the Great Fish of New Zealand. When I was very young I imagined that Maui was very young too and I was very impressed that such a young boy could catch such a great fish.

When I look at my maps of New Zealand, I can see that it is in fact the South Island that is in the shape of a fish. However, I always imagined it was shaped like a shark, not a fish, because when I first heard the story I was terrified of sharks and thought that the shark was the only fish that would fight so violently against Maui's god-like powers.

The Maori name for the North Island is still Te Ika A Maui, meaning the fish-hook of Maui. In other words, Maui used the North Island as his fish-hook to catch the South Island, his Great Fish.

 Maui was, they say, half man and half god. He knew many magic spells and had many magic powers that his older brothers didn't know about, or if they did they pretended to ignore.

One day, when he heard his brothers talking about going fishing, Maui decided that he wanted to go too. So, before his brothers had woken up he went down to where the canoe was, carrying his special fishing hook. Hearing his brothers approach he quickly hid under the floorboards of the boat.

The brothers arrived and they were laughing about having managed to escape without Maui. They were looking forward to having a good day's fishing without being bothered by their young brother.

They pushed out from shore and were still laughing when suddenly they heard a noise.

'What was that?' asked one of them.

Then they thought they heard someone talking. They couldn't see anyone; they couldn't see anything except for the water.

'Oh, it must have been a seagull or something screeching in the distance,' suggested another of the brothers.

Then they heard the sound again. It was Maui, laughing and saying in a strange voice 'I am with you. You haven't tricked me at all.'

The brothers were becoming quite scared now. It sounded like muffled speech but there was no one to be seen.

On they paddled into the deep waters. Again they heard the voice and this time one of the brothers said he thought the noise was coming from under the floorboards so he wrenched up a few. There was Maui, laughing loudly and boasting 'I tricked you! I tricked you!'

The brothers were amazed to see Maui there. They decided to turn back immediately. 'You are not coming with us,' they said. 'You're far too young and our father doesn't want you to come with us.'

But Maui said, 'Look back! Look back to the land! Look how far away it is!'

He had used his magic powers to make the land seem much further away than it really was. The brothers, not realizing that it was a trick, reluctantly agreed to take Maui with them.

They paddled on for a while and then stopped. Just as they were about to throw over the anchor and start their fishing, Maui said, 'No. Please don't do that because I know a much better place further out, full of fish – all the fish you could want. Just a little while longer and you'll have all your nets filled in half the time.'

The brothers were tempted by this promise of fish and paddled out a little further when Maui stopped them and told them to start fishing. So they threw over their nets which within a few minutes were overflowing. They couldn't believe their luck.

Their boat was lying low in the water with the weight of their catch so the brothers told Maui that they were going to turn back. But Maui said, 'No, it's my turn. I haven't had a chance to do my fishing.'

'But we have enough!' they replied.

'No! I want to do my fishing,' insisted Maui.

With that, he pulled out his special fishing hook made of bone, and asked for some bait. The brothers refused to give him any so Maui rubbed his nose so hard that it began to bleed. Then he smeared the hook with his own blood and threw it over the side.

Suddenly the boat was tossed about, and Maui was thrilled because he was sure he had caught a very big fish. He pulled and pulled. The sea was in a turmoil and Maui's brothers sat in stunned silence, marvelling at Maui's magic strength.

Maui heaved and tugged for what seemed like an age until at last the fish broke the surface. Then Maui and his brothers could see that what he

had caught was not a fish but a piece of land, and that his hook was embedded in the doorway of the house of Tonganui, the son of the Sea God.

Maui's brothers couldn't believe their eyes. This beautiful land pulled up from the sea, was smooth and bright, and there were houses on it and burning fires and birds singing. They had never seen anything so marvellous in their whole lives.

Realizing what he had done Maui said, 'I must go and make peace with the gods because I think they are very angry with me. Stay here quietly and calmly, until I return.'

As soon as Maui had gone the brothers forgot his instructions and began to argue for possession of the land.

'I want this piece,' said one.

'No! I claimed it first. It's mine!' shouted another.

Soon the brothers began to slash at the land with their weapons. This angered the gods even more and its smooth surface was gashed and cut. It could never be smoothed out again.

To this day, those cuts and bruises of long ago can still be seen in the valleys and mountains of New Zealand.

Maui Tames
the Sun

Maui had often heard his brothers talking about how there was not enough sunlight during the day. Night after night they would sit round the fire and discuss this problem. No matter how early they got up, still there weren't enough hours of sunlight for all their village duties and for hunting and fishing.

So Maui thought about what he could do to solve their problem. Then he announced to his brothers that he had found a solution: 'I think I can tame the Sun.'

'Maui, don't be so ridiculous!' they replied. 'No one can tame the Sun. For a start, if you got anywhere near him you would be burnt to a cinder. There is no way of taming the Sun. He's far too big and powerful.'

But Maui said, with great authority this time, 'Look, I *can* tame the Sun. Get all the women of the tribe to go and cut as much flax as possible – I want a really huge pile – then I will show you how to make a net that will be strong enough to capture the Sun. I will make sure that he won't go so quickly across the sky in future.'

The brothers obeyed him and when they had collected mounds of flax Maui showed them how to plait it into strong ropes. He made long ropes and short ropes, and tied some of them together to make a net gigantic enough to catch and hold the Sun. After many hours of plaiting they finally had enough rope and nets to please Maui.

Then he set off, equipped with his special axe, with his brothers and some men from the tribe and it took several days to reach the Sun's resting place in the East. After a short stop they started their preparations. They found the cave from which the Sun would be rising next morning and they quickly set to work covering the entrance with the net of plaited ropes. When they were sure they had done a really good job they camouflaged the ropes with leaves and branches. They also made themselves clay walls as a protection against the Sun's fierce heat, and smeared the clay all over their bodies. Then they hid.

Maui crouched down on one side of the cave and the rest of the men were on the other side. It wasn't long before they saw the first glimmer of light from the cave. Then they felt the scorching heat.

The men were shaking with fear as the light grew more and more blinding and the heat more and more stifling. They were sure that Maui's plan would not work. Suddenly they heard a sharp shout from Maui, 'Pull! Pull the ropes as hard as you can.'

The net fell like a huge noose over the Sun. Although the men were terrified that the Sun would kill them all, they pulled and strained as hard as they possibly could so that the Sun could not escape.

The Sun, who was raging at being held captive, struggled and roared. Maui knew he had to do something more than just hold the Sun in the net so he yelled to one of his brothers to take his end of the rope. He rushed out from the protection of his wall and, with his special axe raised high above his head, he ran towards the Sun. Even though the heat was singeing his body and his hair, he started to attack the Sun with his axe.

The Sun roared even louder. 'What are you doing? Are you trying to kill me?' he screamed.

'No. I am not trying to kill you,' answered Maui, 'but you don't understand. You go too fast across the sky, and we are all unable to do our daily work. We need more hours of light in our days for hunting and fishing, for building and repairing our village houses.'

'Well,' said the Sun, 'you have given me such a battering that I don't think I *could* speed across the sky now, even if I wanted to.'

'If we release you,' said Maui, 'will you promise to slow your journey down?'

'You have so weakened me that now I can only go slowly,' answered the Sun.

Maui made him solemnly promise to do what he had asked and then he released the ropes. Maui's brothers and the men of the tribe watched as the Sun, slowly and stiffly, began to lift into the sky. They all smiled at Maui – they were proud of him.

To this day, the Sun travels on his long lonely path across the sky at a very slow pace, giving us many more hours of sunlight than he used to do.

Kupe's Discovery
of Aotearoa

It is well known that Maui fished up the islands of New Zealand from the bottom of the ocean, but it is not so well known that Kupe, who lived in the homeland of Hawaiki, rediscovered them many years later, and called them Aotearoa. This is the story of his adventures.

Kupe was living in Hawaiki and was very much taken with a beautiful young woman called Kura-maro-tini. The trouble was, she was already married to Kupe's cousin, Hoturapa.

Now Kura-maro-tini's father was a great boat-builder. One day, he went into the forest and found a magnificent, tall, straight tree. He cut it down and as it fell it split lengthways into two perfect pieces. He decided to make two strong, beautiful canoes from it; one he called Aotea and gave as a present to his daughter Rongo-rongo, and the other he called Matahorua and gave to his other daughter Kura-maro-tini.

A few days later Kupe went out fishing with his young cousin Hoturapa. When they were anchored far out on the ocean, Kupe's line got snagged. He called to his cousin,

'Come here! Come here and help me!'

Hoturapa came over to him and said,

'Yes, what can I do?'

'I want you to dive under the boat. My line is caught and I don't want to lose it – I went to a lot of trouble to make it, you know, and it's very precious. Would you dive down and free it for me?'

Hoturapa, who wasn't very keen on diving in, tried instead to pull at the line for Kupe but Kupe stopped him.

'No, no, don't bother!' he said. 'I've tried it. It won't shift. Go on, just dive down and free it.'

Hoturapa didn't want to seem unhelpful so he jumped in. As soon as he had disappeared under the surface Kupe cut the anchor rope, threw the rest of his so-called precious line into the water, and paddled like a madman towards land.

By the time Hoturapa surfaced the canoe was already far away and he found himself deserted. Being so far out in the ocean, poor Hoturapa did not stand much of a chance. It was not long before he had drowned, betrayed by his own cousin Kupe.

Kupe, meanwhile, had returned to shore and ran to tell his cousin's family about the tragic 'accident'.

For the moment Kupe thought that his dirty trick had worked and he lost no time in making the beautiful Kura-maro-tini his wife. After a few weeks, though, the families of Hoturapa and Kura-maro-tini grew suspicious about the nature of the fishing accident. Kupe decided it was time for him to leave Hawaiki. He hurriedly prepared Kura's canoe for a long voyage and set off with Kura, his own family and Reti, who was to be priest and navigator, towards that part of the ocean that was called Te Tiritiri o te Moana.

Now, after many, many days of sailing, and not a glimpse of land, the family were becoming very tired and dispirited. Would they ever see land again, they wondered.

Suddenly, early one morning, Kupe's wife called out,

'Look! Look! Land! Land! There's a long white cloud and beneath the cloud I can see land.'

They sailed closer and closer and found that it was a much longer island than any they had ever seen before and that the beautiful white cloud stretched the whole length of it. They called it Aotearoa, Long White Cloud, and there were noisy celebrations in the canoe for the rest of the day.

Kupe decided to navigate all along the coast, to explore all its nooks and crannies. As they were sailing down the east coast of the North Island they came across a small piece of land jutting out into the sea. Kupe could see a large cave in the middle of it. Suddenly, a giant octopus, startled by the approaching canoe with its crew of fierce, tattooed faces, bolted out of the cave and sped away, across the bows of the boat.

Kupe gave chase and followed the octopus until it led him to an

opening between the North Island and the South Island. And so, in this way, Kupe found what is now called Cook Strait.

Kupe sailed on through the Strait and crossed it to explore the land on the other side. The boat was being tossed about by the strong currents and Kupe's family were calling to the gods to give them strength to survive the treacherous seas when, all of a sudden, the octopus emerged from its new hiding place, this time in an angry mood. It raised its tentacles and, with one swift swipe, slammed its suckers against Kupe's boat.

The crew was terrified but Kupe leapt up, grabbed his adze and shouted,

'We must beat this octopus, we must beat it. We have come too far and discovered too much to let this sea creature drag us all down.'

And so the men armed themselves with axes and paddles and a fierce sea battle followed. Kupe slashed at the creature's writhing limbs, slicing bits off them. But still the octopus attacked the boat with what seemed like ever-increasing strength. The crew were even eating the bits that Kupe had sliced off but the octopus did not seem to be weakened in any way. It lashed the water in fury and Kupe and his crew were now in great danger of sinking. Kupe had to think of a way, and quickly, of tricking the octopus.

Dropping his adze, Kupe picked up one of the large gourds that held fresh water. He threw it a short distance away from the boat into the sea. The octopus, thinking it was the body of a man, let go his grip on the canoe and swam towards the gourd. It wrapped its tentacles around the gourd and just then Kupe, who had steered the boat up behind it, raised his adze and with one powerful blow severed the giant octopus in two.

Kupe carried on lashing out with his adze and severed several pieces of land from both the South Island and the North Island. You can still see the islands that Kupe, with his great strength, carved off the main islands.

For a while Kupe rested in the harbour of Tara, Wellington, and there he named two small islands after his daughters Matiu and Makoro. Another daughter Taiapua killed herself and Kupe was distraught. He went to bewail her death at the cliff of Tamure, outside the western heads of the

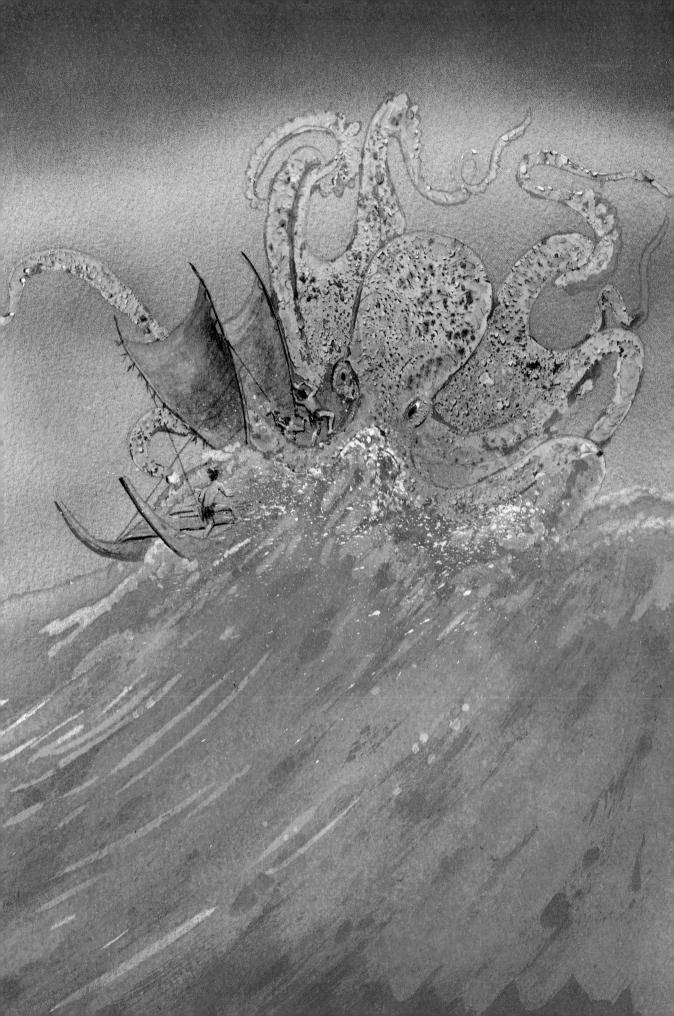

harbour. He cut his forehead with a piece of stone, which was a customary way of showing grief, and his blood stained all the rocks red, as those who pass by today can still see.

After all this Kupe travelled up the west coast to where Patea now stands and marked his visit with a tall post. Here he heard the cry of a kokako and saw the little tiwaiwaka flitting about in the beautiful trees and fanning out its black-and-white tail. Now it was time to return to his own land, to Hawaiki.

So Kupe made the long, difficult voyage back and told his people about the land of the great white clouds and high mists. When he was asked if he had found any people there he answered,

'I saw the kokako and the little tiwaiwaka.'

A direct 'no' might have sounded rude, he thought.

Then Kupe was asked if he would return one day to Aotearea. Again he avoided the blunt 'no'.

'E hoki Kupe? Will Kupe return?' was his reply.

To this day, 'E hoki Kupe' is sometimes used as a Maori way of politely saying 'no'.

Hinemoa and Tutanekai

When I think of Lake Rotorua in the middle of the North Island of New Zealand I see it at night. As a child I used to go there quite often and watch the silver moon shining over the water. It never seemed to be a rough or difficult lake – always rippling. Seeing the island of Mokoia in the middle of it I always picture Hinemoa swimming to her hero, her warrior, Tutanekai, and I always imagined her as a kind of fairy princess. This is her story.

 There was once a very handsome warrior called Tutanekai who used to hunt and fish with his step-brothers on their island home of Mokoia. From time to time he would daydream about the woman he would marry. But winning a bride would not be easy: his step-brothers were serious rivals and they were always boasting that they would marry the most beautiful of women and have the most children.

On the mainland there was a legendary beauty called Hinemoa. Her father was a very great but gruff warrior, and he adored Hinemoa. He would not let anybody, not anybody at all, marry his Hinemoa. Many handsome chiefs had come to him to ask for her hand in marriage, but not one of them was good enough for his daughter.

Now the tribes sometimes gathered on the mainland for meetings and on these occasions there was much competition as to who had the most land or the biggest house for Hinemoa.

One day Hinemoa and Tutanekai caught sight of each other at one of these tribal gatherings. They could not speak to each other, as Hinemoa's father made sure that she was protected from the advances of any of the young men. But they had seen each other and that was enough: it was love at first sight. Once the tribes had all returned to their homes Hinemoa began to think about Tutanekai, night after night.

Tutanekai was something of a loner. He was most at peace when he could go off on his own and play his flute. As soon as he returned home he felt sure that Hinemoa was the love of his dreams. She really was the most beautiful girl with her long wavy hair, round olive face and dark brown eyes.

Night after night Tutanekai would think of Hinemoa and give voice to his emotions on the flute. Everyone in her tribe would listen to this music, but most of all Hinemoa would listen to its soulful, haunting sounds. It made her feel sad and once again she would think of Tutanekai, far away on the island of Mokoia. Little did she know that this was his music.

Time passed and there were several tribal gatherings. The more Tutanekai came to these meetings and Hinemoa saw him, the more they fell in love with each other.

One day Hinemoa and Tutanekai finally had a few moments together alone, and although they were very shy they knew that their love for each other was growing all the time. Hinemoa felt Tutanekai's great strength and she felt the protection of his powerful body and kind, handsome face.

Tutanekai wondered how they might persuade her father to agree to their marriage. Hinemoa was terrified.

'No,' she cried 'this has happened so many times that I cannot see my father ever giving permission for us to get married.'

Tutanekai said, 'Look, we are in love, we *should* be married! Come to my island of Mokoia with me.'

'It is not possible,' replied Hinemoa. 'They would see us and bring me back to Rotorua and I would *never* be allowed to see you again, ever!'

But Tutanekai was determined. He said, 'No, you are to be mine. I want you as my wife. I have a plan. When your tribe is sleeping and I am back in Mokoia you must go down to the water's edge and push out a canoe and paddle it to me.'

'But how will I find you? How will I find the island of Mokoia?'

'I have a flute,' said Tutanekai. 'I play my music every night.'

'So that's *your* flute! After all these nights, I didn't realize it was your music playing to me. Of course I know where you are. I've known where you've been for so many days and nights now. Yes! I *do* have the courage. I will be able to find you.'

Tutanekai returned to his island with his step-brothers and his father, and Hinemoa waited. That night there was no moon. When she heard the flute she rushed down to the water's edge to find a canoe. But there was none. She could not find a single one. They were all high up on the shore. It was impossible for her to push one down, even though she tried and tried again – the canoes were very heavy and she was not strong enough.

Frustrated, she crept back to her sleeping mat and cried herself to sleep, thinking 'I can hear the sound of the flute and I can't come to you. I will try again tomorrow night.'

The following night the moon was still hidden and when darkness fell Hinemoa once again heard her lover's flute. It was time to go. She rushed down to the water's edge. Impossible! Not a single canoe could she find.

Night after night the same thing happened. With the sound of Tutanekai's music floating over the water Hinemoa became desperate. She must get to Mokoia. She decided to go without the help of a canoe. During the day she found some dried gourds and hid them away. That night she went down to the water clutching the gourds and, without even glancing back, she tied the gourds together and floated them on the water. Then she lay on them and pushed herself out into the dark lake. She started to paddle in the direction of the flute playing. The music guided her through the moonless night and although she was exhausted, she kept on paddling.

She was getting nearer to Mokoia but the cold water had chilled her to the bone and she began to feel very weak. The music sounded faint now but all the same it gave her courage to press on. Suddenly she felt as if she might be within shouting distance of the island. She put a foot down in the water and touched some waving weed. A moment later she felt solid land and climbed, stiffly, out of the water.

Terrified of the darkness and the stillness, she took a few hesitant steps on to the dry land which felt warm under her feet. The rest of her body still felt cold – she was quite naked as she had thrown off her cloak when she plunged in. The warm rocks reminded her of the geysers back on the mainland. As she walked a little further the land became hotter and soon Hinemoa caught the welcome sound of hissing water. Geysers! A few steps further and she found herself beside a beautiful pool of hot sulphurous water. She lowered herself in and lay there, soaking up the warmth.

She lay for quite some time, and gradually her fingers and toes felt like they belonged to her once again. She wondered what she should do.

'Now, I know Tutanekai is here, but I can't go down to the village with just my hair covering my body! I must find a way of making him come to me.'

Just then she heard footsteps, so she lay very still. As they came closer she called out, disguising her voice,

'Who is there?'

A terrified voice answered 'Who is that?'

Then Hinemoa called out again, 'What are you doing here?'

The same voice blurted out, 'I am getting water for my master, Tutanekai.'

'Give me the water bag,' demanded Hinemoa.

Hinemao could just make out the shape of a man holding a bag at arm's length. As soon as she reached out to take it he ran off. She had a drink and then sank back into the pool. What should she do now?

Soon she heard more voices. She lay very quietly and saw a large shadow approaching the pool. She began to panic. 'On no!' she thought, 'it's a monster. Something terrible will happen to me and I will never see Tutanekai again.' She closed her eyes, hoping it would disappear. When she opened them, she couldn't believe what she saw: there was Tutanekai, who also could not believe his eyes, standing right before her.

'Hinemoa,' he said, 'How did you get here? How long have you been here?'

Once Hinemoa had recovered from the shock of seeing Tutanekai, she told him the story of her flight from the mainland, and how terrified she was of the cold water, and how this beautiful, hot, bubbling pool seemed to have been put there specially for her comfort and warmth.

When she had finished Tutanekai said, 'Come quickly. While it is still dark I will take you down to my village. There we'll find some clothing for you.'

They went to his hut and talked and talked for most of the night about their love for each other and their desire to spend the rest of their lives together.

The next morning, when the rest of Tutanekai's family were up and about, there was no sign of Tutanekai. 'Why isn't he here?' they asked. So they sent one of the servants to rouse him, who soon rushed back saying 'I cannot believe it! There is someone else with Tutanekai, and I . . . I . . . they are both asleep in there, and it's . . . it's a *woman*, a woman there with Tutanekai!'

The rest of the tribe looked at each other, amazed. Could there be a stranger in the village? They had not heard anyone come into the village

in the night. And why had Tutanekai not told them about this stranger, this woman?

They were just about to dispatch the same servant to find out who this stranger was, when Tutanekai and Hinemoa appeared, walking towards them. As soon as Tutanekai's family saw their radiant faces they knew that they were in love. They knew, too, that this beautiful woman was Hinemoa.

All of Tutanekai's tribe were happy for them but were also worried about what Hinemoa's father would do. He might declare war on them, they said, in order to get his daughter back. So that day they sent a group of warriors to him. They told him that Hinemoa was safe and asked him to agree to her marriage with Tutanekai.

At first Hinemoa's father was annoyed, but he soon relented, realizing how his brave daughter had suffered so for the love of her warrior Tutanekai.

Throughout the whole area there was great feasting, night after night, and Hinemoa and Tutanekai were finally married. To this day the warm bubbling pool where Hinemoa revived herself is known as Hinemoa's Bath.

Kahukura and
the Fairies

The Maori people of long ago believed in fairy spirits who were tall and white-skinned. They were people of the night, sometimes dangerous, and it was said that if the sun touched their bodies they would die. I never believed that they died if they were exposed to sunlight, rather that they were doomed to return to the caves where I imagined they lived, never to leave them again.

The Maori word for the fairies is patupaiarehe. Although the story tellers spoke of both male and female fairies I always imagined them as female, and very beautiful too.

Kahukura was a young chief who was worried about his tribe because food was very scarce where they lived on the west coast of the North Island. While everyone else, his friends and brothers and the young men of the tribe, were out fishing and hunting, trying to gather food for the tribe, Kahukura stayed at home.

He would spend much of his time just looking out to sea, as if in a daydream. He felt his mission in life was to find a way of helping his tribe out of their troubles. He kept staring at the ocean, thinking about all the food that it held. How could they harvest more from it, he wondered.

The old men of the tribe would look at him, standing on the shore, and say, 'He is daydreaming and waiting for something to come out of the ocean. We just don't understand him!'

Kahukura continued to daydream but seemed very sure of himself and sure that soon he would be able to help his tribe. Each night he dreamt of going north, of some force that was drawing him to the north of the North Island. A voice would whisper, 'Come, come we have much to tell you up here.'

Night after night he would dream that he was walking and walking, further and further north, until he reached a beautiful sandy beach where the glittering water dazzled him and strange music echoed all around.

One evening he was watching his friends dancing and singing when he heard a voice. At first it was just a whisper. But then he could hear it clearly and it was saying, 'Come, come north. Come to Rangiaowhia.'

He had never even heard of Rangiaowhia but he could feel a strange magnetic power in the voice that was repeating 'Come north' over and over again.

So he did. He set out alone, without telling anybody.

It was a long, tough trek. There were no paths for him to follow so he cut across the land, through forests, over waterfalls and through thorny scrub. He was drenched by rain but never gave a moment's thought to turning back for he was convinced that there was something waiting for him that would be good for his tribe and for their future.

Late one afternoon he came over a rise and saw, below him, a beautiful sandy beach, the very beach of his dreams. He felt a certain glow and comfort now that he had reached his destination. But he was puzzled: why had he been drawn to this beach which only seemed to contain rocks, sand and water? He couldn't understand it.

He walked down onto the beach and looked around. He found a few sticks, a bit of dried flax and a pile of fish bones and guts. It looked as if some people had been gutting fish there. But the only footsteps Kahukura could discover were his own. Then he thought that perhaps the tide had washed up all these things. But no, he told himself, the water hadn't come up that far. Kahukura was even more puzzled.

He sat beside a rock. Maybe by sitting and waiting, he thought, I will discover why there are no footprints. He was so tired after his long journey that he very soon fell asleep. When he woke several hours later, it was night and the moon was shining brightly. For a moment he could not work out where he was. Then he heard strange, haunting music, the same music as in his dreams. But this time he was awake, and the music was getting louder and louder.

He could see the water glittering, but the glittering was not caused by the moonlight but by torches, and it was moving nearer and nearer to the land. Clutching his greenstone axe for protection, Kahukura crept down to the water's edge.

Now he could make out two canoes and he could hear voices. There was a strange sort of rope stretched between the canoes and the voices were calling to each other and giving instructions, 'Pull in the net! Pull in the net!'

Kahukura, who only knew about the spears and baited lines that were used in his tribe, had never heard of a 'net' and he wondered if this could be a new fishing device. He was fascinated, and he crept even closer to see what they were doing.

'Pull in the net!' the voices cried again.

As they were pulling, the fish were jumping and flapping inside the net. Kahukura had never seen so many fish. Now that he could see these people more clearly he realized that their skin was much fairer than his. Suddenly he knew that he was in the midst of a group of fairies and that this beach was where they landed their fish at night. Now he understood why there were no footprints in the sand.

The fairies were so busy with the task of getting in their haul that they didn't notice that Kahukura was not one of them. He watched them dragging the bulging net up onto the sand and then he slipped in beside them to lend a hand. He was determined to find how this net worked. How could the fairies pull the net along in the water without the fish escaping? What a gift this would be for his own people, Kahukura thought.

Since the fairies couldn't carry home all the fish in the net, they started to knot pieces of flax at one end and then string them through the gills of the fish. In that way, each fairy could carry a chain of fish. Kahukura joined in but he did not tie the knot at the end, and so the fish slipped off. The fairies came to help him, but time and time again, when their backs were turned, he undid the knot and the fish fell off. Kahukura knew that once night had passed and the sun started to rise the fairies were in great danger, so they would be racing to pack their catch before dawn. By untying his knot he was delaying them most effectively.

All this time he kept a watchful eye on the eastern sky which was gradually lightening. The fairies were being urged by their chief to hurry. They were still picking up the last of the fish when the sun came up. In the one brief moment when they saw that Kahukura was not one of them the sunlight lit their bodies, and they vanished.

All that was left was just a few fish and the net, this magical net that Kahukura now realized was the meaning behind his dream: he was supposed to find it and take it back to his tribe.

Kahukura packed up the net very carefully and started his long

journey back. He studied the net each day to discover how it was made and how it worked. By the time he arrived home he had solved its puzzle.

His family and friends rushed up to him and said, 'Where have you been? Why were you away so long? We were worried about you. We thought you were dead.'

But Kahukura only smiled and brought out of his sack the fairy fishing net. They would no longer have to rely on baited lines and spears for catching fish, he explained. And he began to show them his wonderful new discovery.

The Talking
Taniwha
of Rotorua

A taniwha is a monster which usually lurks in deep water or under cliffs and rocks. When I was young, I heard about one particular taniwha and it frightened the life out of me.

There was a fruit tree growing by a bridge under which there lived a taniwha. Now the taniwha believed the fruit belonged to him. One day a young boy took the fruit to eat and was swept into the river and drowned. I am not sure whether or not the taniwha deliberately drowned the boy but from then on I was always terrified of taking fruit from any tree, especially from one that was beside a bridge and a lot of running water!

The talking taniwha of Rotorua was supposed to have been a black monster with a great head and bat-like wings that stretched twelve feet from tip to tip. Although the taniwha was often thought of as a fishy type of beast I have always imagined it to be like a dragon, with scales, and jaws filled with sharp teeth.

There was once an enormous, man-eating taniwha who ruled supreme on one side of a mountain in Rotorua, and it was very difficult to get from one side to the other without crossing his path. A Waikato chief, who was called Kahu-ki-te-rangi, was in love with Koka, daughter of another chief called Pou-whenua who lived on the Rotorua side of the mountain. Now Kahu knew that the people of Rotorua wanted to be able to pass safely from one side of the mountain to the other along a mountain track without having to make a tiring detour. Kahu was also longing to see more of Koka. So, he tried to figure out a way of getting rid of the taniwha or of making a good track that was well out of the taniwha's reach.

One day Kahu went the long way round to visit Koka and he explained to Pou-whenua that he wanted to get rid of the taniwha and make a track around the mountain so that both tribes could move freely and swiftly from one side to the other. The old chief, who was no fool, thought that this was rather a generous offer so he said to Kahu, 'On what condition?'

'I want your daughter to be my wife,' replied Kahu.

Pou-whenua was happy to agree to this: it would be a very good marriage and the people of Rotorua and Waikato would together remove

the threat of their common enemy, the taniwha, who had been plaguing them for as long as he could remember. Kahu returned home to get his people ready for the task of making a proper track.

Now Kahu was already one step ahead of everybody else because he had been taught all about taniwhas by his father who was a noted taniwha killer. He had even learned the language of the taniwha. He also knew that this particular taniwha had a special weakness for having his back scratched. So Kahu went to the taniwha's lair and he was not afraid.

He walked straight in and started talking. The taniwha was so taken aback that he forgot all about his appetite for human flesh and when Kahu started to scratch his back he began to feel quite hospitable.

The taniwha and Kahu talked. Kahu was very persuasive.

'Now, come on,' he said. 'I think you should think of taking a wife and going away from this place.'

The taniwha was puzzled by Kahu's suggestion. 'What do you mean?' he asked.

'Well, I think I can find a wife for you.'

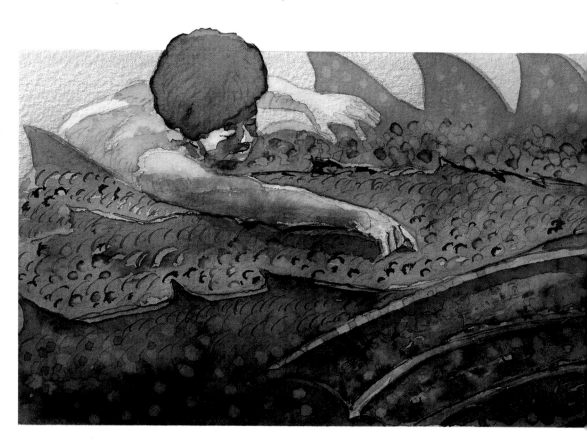

At this, the taniwha began to show some interest. But he was still cautious.

'But, why do you want me to leave this place and go to the other side? You're the only one who dares to use this route.'

'Oh, well,' Kahu replied, 'if I find you a wife you'll be much happier on the other side. But you must promise me that you will stay there.'

The taniwha thought it sounded quite tempting.

'What sort of a wife?' he asked.

'I will find a Waikato woman for you within two days,' said Kahu, 'but only if you promise to keep your side of the bargain, and stay on the other side of the mountain.'

The taniwha agreed and Kahu left, pleased with his scheme.

Kahu knew that it would be difficult to match someone up with the taniwha but he had an old woman in mind. She was really ugly and good for only one thing – burying the dead. None of the rest of the tribe would have anything to do with her. She was called Pukaka.

Kahu sought her out and told her that he had found her a husband.

The old woman, who was hideously filthy, with matted hair and rags for clothes, refused to believe him.

'What do you mean?' she said.' Found *me* a husband? No one in their right mind would offer to find me a husband.'

'*I* have found you a husband, 'replied Kahu. 'He is waiting for you.'

'Where?'

'On the hill, between here and Rotorua.'

'But there is only a taniwha living there,' said Pukaka.

'That's right. It's the taniwha that wants to marry you. He has agreed to be your husband and to provide for you.'

The old woman thought to herself, Well, life here is miserable. At least I will have a husband for company and the home of a taniwha is better than starving to death.

So Pukaka said she would go with Kahu and he led her along the path to the taniwha's lair.

The taniwha and the old woman looked at each other and they were not particularly pleased with what they saw. But, at least they would have each other. The taniwha said he would take Pukaka and would make the best of a bad bargain.

Kahu drew Pukaka to one side. 'Now, don't forget,' he said, 'give his back a good scratch and then he'll do anything for you. For the sake of your people, see that he remains on the other side of the mountain.'

When Kahu left the taniwha kept to his word, put Pukaka on his back and flew to the other side of the mountain and settled down with his new bride.

With the taniwha gone the Waikato men could get to work on their track. They cut down trees and flattened the undergrowth. When they had finished it was a good wide track for both the tribes to travel on. Now Kahu and his friends were able to go to Rotorua much more speedily than before, without any fear of the taniwha.

Kahu was married to Koka and the ceremony lasted for many, many days. Once the festivities were over Kahu and Koka and all the Waikato people started their journey back. The pace was slow as they were all exhausted from the celebrations and from lack of sleep. Unknown to them the taniwha had broken his promise and had returned. He was hiding in the ferns, watching the long straggling line of wedding guests.

The taniwha was not at all happy. As he heard sounds of laughter and saw Kahu escorting the beautiful Koka he began to ask himself why he couldn't have a young, beautiful wife instead of his ugly Pukaka. He grew more and more angry as he thought of his hideous old Pukaka whom Kahu had tricked him into accepting. He decided to take his revenge.

As the Waikato people passed by his hiding place the taniwha rushed out and grabbed four beautiful young women, one of whom was Koka. He soared up over the trees and flew back to his old lair further up the mountain to prepare to feast on these tender young women.

Kahu was distraught. He saw what was happening but could do nothing about it. He could not fly after the taniwha. In anger he gathered all the members of his tribe and told them that they must get rid of the vicious creature, once and for all. They made a plan.

They made a special flax rope which they carried to the entrance of the taniwha's cave where they shaped it into a noose and propped it up in a forked stick. The ends of the rope trailed into the trees on either side of the cave where Kahu's people hid themselves, and made ready to grab hold of each end of the rope when the signal was given.

Kahu strode out of the forest and stood in broad daylight, in the clearing in front of the cave. This time, he was distinctly nervous, but he stood his ground and roared at the taniwha.

'Come out of there, you coward, you breaker of promises.'

The taniwha's head appeared.

'Ah, it's you, Kahu! Do you want to see my new wife, Koka, she is so young and pretty? Or maybe you would prefer Pukaka – she's all yours, over there on the other side of the mountain.'

The taniwha was very pleased with himself. He carried on taunting Kahu.

'Koka is in my cave, waiting patiently for me. Don't you worry about her, I'm looking after her.'

Kahu was incensed. 'You've stolen my wife, you vile creature, and now I am going to take her back from you.'

The taniwha just laughed.

'Ha, you would need an army to get her away from here. I have magic powers and am a hundred times stronger than any one of your puny people. You had better get going, now, or I will grab you and squeeze the life out of you and then throw you to the birds.'

Kahu made no reply. Instead, he stuck out his tongue, and the

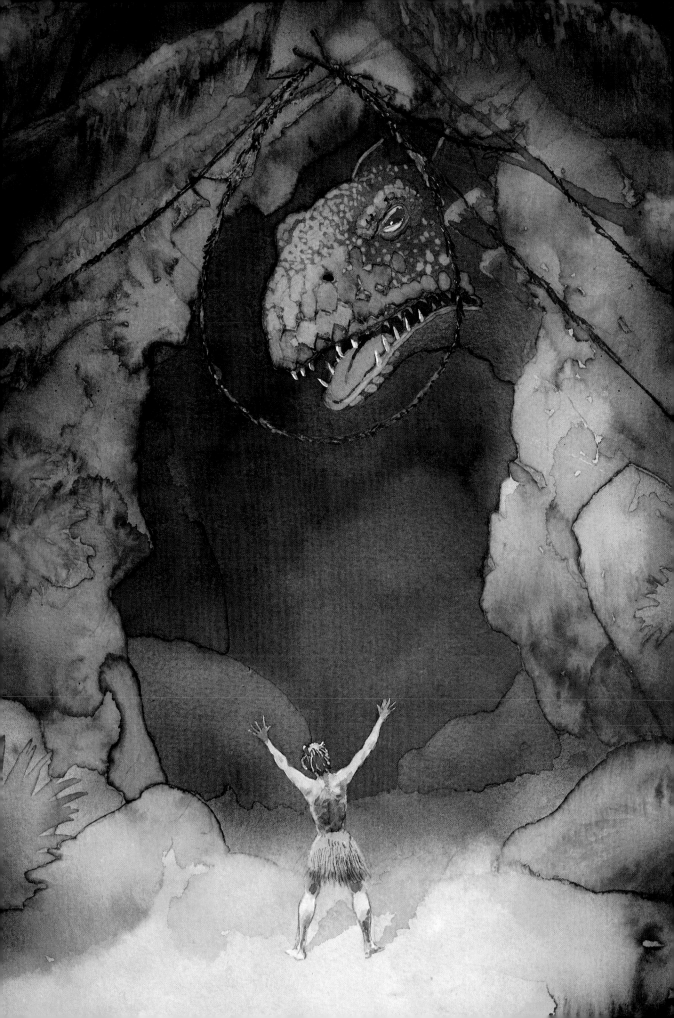

taniwha was so enraged by this gesture that he rushed out at Kahu. Kahu beat a hasty retreat, turning round a couple of times to stick out his tongue again which infuriated the taniwha further. He dodged past the noose, shouting at his friends to snatch the pole away as soon as the taniwha drew level with it.

The taniwha blundered right into the noose and instantly a hundred hands at each side of it pulled and pulled. The taniwha was caught, mid flight, and could not escape. As the noose tightened it bit into his neck and choked him to death.

Kahu tore up the hill to rescue Koka from the cave. He comforted and calmed her, telling her of the taniwha's death. Both their tribes could now live in peace and safety.

Kahu was the hero of the day, and from then on was known as the new taniwha killer of the region.

Te Kanawa
and the Visitors
by Firelight

When I was a child I was told many stories about the great Waikato chief, Te Kanawa, and he was always described as a very handsome man. Sometimes he was the strongest and sometimes the most envied man in the tribe as well.

This story tells how the patupaiarehe, or fairies, having heard that Te Kanawa was so handsome and strong, came to see for themselves.

One day, Te Kanawa decided to go out hunting for kiwi as he needed feathers for a new cloak. He waited until dusk, for kiwis are nocturnal, and set off with some friends and his hunting dogs.

Te Kanawa was out of luck for there was no moon that night and in the blackness it was impossible to find any kiwi. So he suggested that they should all bed down for the night. They found themselves a huge pukatea tree, with thick roots that broke the surface of the earth, and made their fire at the foot of it. They laid down their warm cloaks in the spaces in between the roots and settled down for the night.

Just as they were dropping off to sleep they heard loud voices, as if a big crowd of people was moving through the forest in their direction. Te Kanawa looked up but all he could see were the shadows thrown out by the fire. The noise was increasing as if it was coming closer and closer all the time. Suddenly Te Kanawa shouted 'Patupaiarehe! They have come down from the mountains.'

Instantly there was panic among the young warriors as they all threw themselves flat on the ground, pulling their cloaks over them. Only the dogs remained calm. They slept on, deaf to the sound of the approaching fairies. Te Kanawa, however, conscious of his position as leader, did not

cover his head but peered bravely into the darkness to see if he could make out any of the intruders. Suddenly, they were all round him, walking over his warriors, walking over the dogs.

The men were shaking under their cloaks. They did not dare face the fairies in case they might accidently do anything to disturb or offend them. They knew that fairies can do terrible things to men, especially if they use their magic spells.

Te Kanawa could hear the fairies chanting as they gathered around to look at him.

'We've come to the mountain, over the mountain Tirangi, to see the handsome chief, Te Kanawa.'

He didn't know what to do. Naturally he couldn't tell them to go away, for fear of displeasing them. Yet the sooner he could get rid of them the better. Then Te Kanawa thought of his precious greenstone jewels. If he offered those to the fairies they might be persuaded to leave.

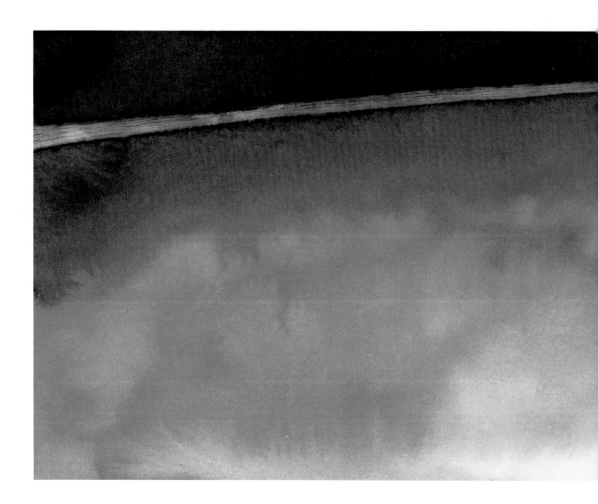

So, he took off the beautiful piece of greenstone hanging round his neck and showed it to them. The fairies chattered excitedly, but they would not touch it. Then Te Kanawa took off his shark's tooth earring and his long greenstone earring to show them.

Suddenly, a log fell out of the fire and a tongue of flame shot up into the dark night. In the blink of an eye the fairies had vanished. But as the flame died down they crept back from their hiding places to take another look at the jewels.

By this time Te Kanawa was desperate to get rid of his visitors but was afraid of being touched by them. So he found a long stick, hung the pendant and earrings on the end of it and stretched it out for the fairies to take the jewels. To his amazement, instead of reaching for the jewels the fairy leader bent down and picked up the shadows that the pendant and earrings had made on the ground. Then he handed these shadows round to each of his people and they examined them with exclamations of

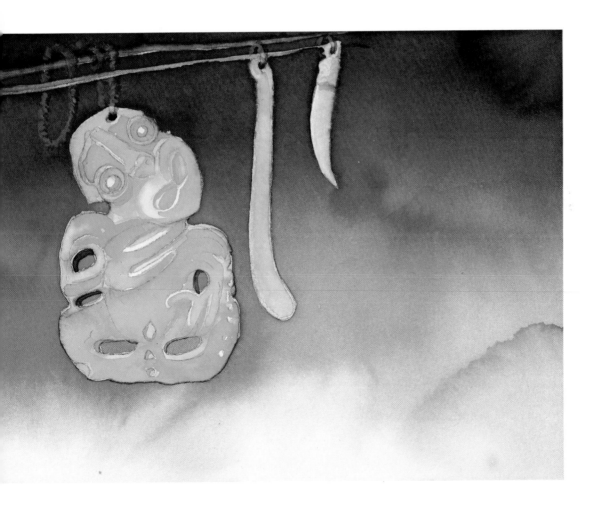

delight. Then, when all of them had touched the shadows the whole troop disappeared, taking the shadows with them.

Te Kanawa lay down, pulled his cloak over his head and tried to go back to sleep. But his heart was beating so fast that he could not sleep at all.

At first light he jumped up and went over to inspect the stick: his pendant and earrings were still hanging there.

He roused the men.

'We have had a narrow escape,' he told them. And they fled that place, without a backward glance.

Mataora and Niwareka in the Underworld

This is the story about learning the art of moko, the Maori word for tattooing.

———————————

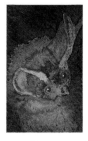 Mataora was a great warrior chief and his people were very proud of him and of the many wars he had fought. One night, after much festivities, Mataora went to sleep and was having a wonderful dream about being in a fight and being cheered and hailed by his people. Although it was only a dream, Mataora could see them clearly and could hear their shouts of encouragement.

Just as he felt that he was winning the fight he realized he was dreaming and that the dream was fading. At that same moment he sensed that he was being watched, not in his dream but in real life. As he opened his eyes he heard laughter and as his eyes focused he could make out a circle of white faces, all staring at him.

Nervously, he cried out, 'Who are you? What are you?'

Laughing, they replied, 'We are the Turehu.'

And now Mataora could see that they were all women, their blonde hair framing their beautiful, pale faces. They smiled and said,

'We are from Rarohenga, the Underworld. But what are you? A god?'

'Why do you ask who I am and what I am? I am a man. Can you not see that for yourselves?' said Mataora, a little annoyed.

'But you are not tattooed in the way of our people,' they said.

'What do you mean?' he replied. 'I *am* tattooed. These designs on my face are tattoos.'

'No,' they insisted, 'the real tattoo is one that you can't wipe off. A child could wipe off yours.'

'Well,' said Mataora, his temper rising, 'what other way is there?'

But they would not give him a direct answer. All they said was, 'One day, you might find out.'

Now Mataora was fascinated by this visit from the Turehu for no one had ever seen them before in his part of the country. Adopting the role of courteous host he asked them to sit down and share a meal with him.

'Yes, we would like to eat, but we would prefer to eat outside and not in your hut,' they answered.

So Mataora went to his storehouse and brought back quantities of cooked food and laid it all out before them. The Turehu, however, just looked at it. Although Mataora thought that the food looked very appetizing these strange people did not want to eat it. Mataora asked them why they did not eat.

'This food is bad,' they said.

Now Mataora, who had tried very hard to give them his best food from the storehouse, began to lose patience with the Turehu.

'I will eat it!' he said, 'I will eat it before your very eyes!'

And as he ate some of it, the Turehu crowded round him and watched his every move. Then they whispered amongst themselves.

'Well, he is still alive!'

They watched as he ate more and one of them even prized open his mouth to see where the food had gone.

Mataora suddenly realized what all this fuss was about. The Turehu, he now remembered, were said to like only raw food.

That's no problem, he said to himself, and he got up and went down to his little pond where he kept fresh fish for special occasions, such as this. He caught several and laid them in front of the fair-skinned people. They laughed with delight and helped themselves.

While they were eating Mataora had a chance to study them more closely. They were an elegant people, very tall, and with quite thin noses. They wore waistmats of dried seaweed and sat gracefully erect. He noticed that they laughed a lot, and imagined it was because they felt shy in the company of an Overworld person.

One young girl, in particular, caught Mataora's eye: she was taller than the others and very beautiful, and seemed to be glancing in his direction. He was just thinking that he would like to get to know her better when she came over and sat next to him. They just looked at each other, without speaking. As the day wore on she became more pleasing to him, and he became more pleasing to her.

Mataora decided to entertain his guests with a dance, a dance worthy of a warrior and a chief. So he jumped up and whirled around, dancing, and the Turehu were delighted, particularly the beautiful girl. When he sat down the Turehu all joined together in a stately dance, quite different to any other that Mataora had ever seen. The tall girl came to the front and wove with her feet a small pattern in the sand. The others joined hands and followed her, weaving in and out of each others' intertwined arms. Mataora grew quite dizzy watching them; he was so mesmerized by the beauty of their dance that he decided to ask his visitors if he could choose a wife.

They stopped dancing and rushed towards him saying,

'Yes! Which one of us do you want?'

He pointed to the tall girl who was standing a little way off. She now seemed overcome with shyness. But as the others made space for her she slowly came forwards and stood right in front of him. They pressed noses. He took her hands and they looked into each other's eyes. Mataora was very happy: they would be bound together for the rest of their lives. Her name was Niwareka.

They were married there and then and the Turehu all danced and feasted. When the wedding was over Mataora's new bride said,

'I am the daughter of Ue-tonga of the Underworld, but now I belong to you, Mataora, great chief of the Overworld.'

And they were both very happy.

Over the next few days the Turehu disappeared and went back to their world, leaving Mataora and Niwareka alone to get on with their lives in the Overworld village. Mataora loved his wife dearly, and as the days passed his love grew and grew. But something was wrong and they both knew it.

Mataora had a terrible temper and as Niwareka was such a gentle person and was away from her family, she was frightened by his outbursts. One day, he lost his temper once too often, and struck her. Niwareka was devastated by this. It was something she had never experienced or even seen in the Underworld. She was so distressed that later that night she left Mataora's hut and slipped away into the darkness.

Mataora woke the next morning and discovered that she had disappeared. He remembered striking her but thought that she would know that it was only one of his usual bouts of temper. He waited all day for Niwareka to return, and when she didn't he became worried and decided to look for her. And as he set out, he began to realize the terrible thing he had done.

Although it was bright daylight everything seemed black before his eyes because he was so distraught. He loved Niwareka so much and wanted to tell her how sorry he was.

He guessed that she would have gone back to her home in Rarohenga and so he headed that way, even though he knew there could be dangers. Presently he came to the House of the Four Winds where the spirits of the dead make their entrance to Rarohenga. The guardian of the House was standing outside so he asked him,

'Have you seen a young woman pass by this way?'

'What does she look like?' the guardian asked.

'She is very tall, with blonde hair and fair skin, and she is very beautiful.'

'Ah!' the guardian said. 'Yes, a young woman who was crying did rush past me here a while ago.'

Mataora knew straightaway that it must have been his Niwareka.

'You may follow,' continued the guardian, 'if you have the courage, and this is the way.'

He opened the door and Mataora saw a dark tunnel, leading downwards. He lowered himself into it and the door was shut firmly behind him. There wasn't a glimmer of light anywhere. For a moment Mataora thought that this was a trap, that no one would ever find him and that he would certainly never find Niwareka. But, remembering the guardian's words about courage, he pressed on.

As he stumbled and fell down the tunnel, all he could think of was finding Niwareka. Suddenly he saw a half light, and then a fantail fluttering about. The fantail was always a good sign so he felt encouraged.

'Follow me, follow me,' it called, 'I will keep you safe!'

Mataora asked the fantail if it had seen a beautiful young lady with long flaxen hair and pale skin.

'Yes, I have seen her,' the fantail replied. 'Her eyes were red and she was very sad. She was weeping.'

So Mataora rushed on again. Soon he came to the end of the tunnel and out into a new world. There was no sun, but there was plenty of light. He could not make out where it was coming from for there was no sky, only a roof that seemed to be made out of rocks. But everything seemed to be bathed in light; it seemed to fill every nook and cranny. Birds were singing and there were trees and grass and a breeze, just like in the real world. Mataora knew that this must be the Underworld.

In the distance he could make out a man lying on the ground and another man bending over him. He walked up to them and watched. The man lying down was young and seemed to be in agony; the man bending over him was older and was holding a fine bone chisel and tapping it into the face of the younger one. The chisel was chipping out a narrow path across his face and blood was streaming out of the wound, and yet the young man did not cry or shout. Mataora watched the torture that was being inflicted on him, and he could not understand what was happening.

From time to time the man with the chisel would stop what he was doing to give the young man a rest from the pain. Mataora looked at the two men, and they were silent.

'I am Mataora,' he said.

'I am Ue-tonga,' the older man replied.

And they fell silent again: there was nothing more to be said. For a long time Mataora sat there, observing the man's artistry with the chisel. At length, he spoke to Ue-tonga again.

'What are you doing? Will the face ever come back? Will the face ever mend?'

Ue-tonga replied, 'Yes, it will. This is the way we do the moko, this is the way we do the tattoo.'

'No!' said Mataora. 'My tattoo is the true moko and it is put on with paint. Look at it!'

Ue-tonga leaned forward and touched Mataora's face and with one firm sweep of his hand he wiped off his tattoo. Mataora screamed. 'Oh no! What's happened to my tattoo! Now you must put it back on my face.'

Suddenly he heard laughter, the laughter of the young women, and, for a minute, he thought that he was back in his hut, dreaming about fighting to the death. He looked around, and they were all there, the same faces, the same fair-haired people. He looked for Niwareka but he couldn't see her. Where could she be?

Ue-tonga, who had finished with the young man for the day, said,

'Your moko is useless, it is only painted. Now I will put the real moko on your face.'

So Mataora lay down, and, with a piece of charcoal, Ue-tonga sketched the design for the moko on his face. Mataora closed his eyes and lay there, knowing that it was going to be very painful. Ue-tonga started chiselling, and the pain was excruciating. Mataora could feel the drops of blood running down his face onto his body and he knew that he must be brave if he wanted to have his moko back. He knew that he must lie there for as long as he could bear because the new moko was special – it would stay on his face for the rest of his life.

Ue-tonga was a great master at the particular moko that he was now creating for Mataora. The intricate patterns, twirls and swirls that he

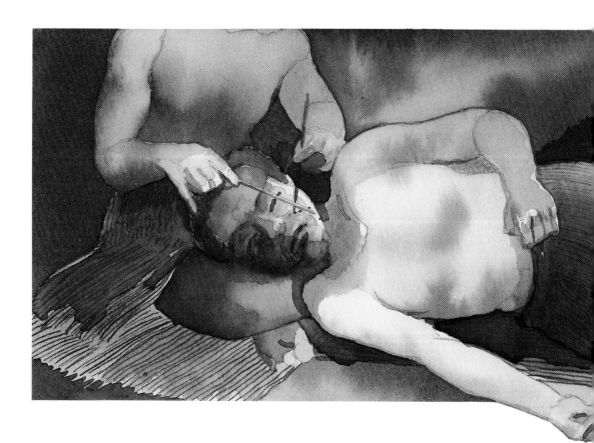

used on the warriors' faces made them look both frightening and beautiful.

All Mataora could hear, as he lay there in agony, was the tap-tapping of the chisel, creeping slowly across his face. All he could think of was to call out to Niwareka in the hope that she would hear him. And so he called her name, over and over again, and the wind carried his voice across the Underworld.

A younger sister of Niwareka heard the voice and rushed to see where it came from. She ran to where her sister was and said,

'There is someone, lying over there on the ground, with your father Ue-tonga, and he is calling your name. He is being tattooed and he seems to know you.'

Niwareka went straight to where her father was and she saw a young man lying there, and while she could not recognize his face because it was swollen and covered in blood, she thought she recognized the body. And Mataora, who by this time could not take any more of the tattooing, stood up. His eyes were so swollen that he could not see Niwareka, and he kept calling her name.

She stood before him and said in a quiet voice,

'Mataora, it is you, isn't it?'

Mataora recognized her voice. He held out his arms and she knew that he was indeed her husband. They embraced and wept for joy that they had been joined together again.

When the tattooing was finished and the wounds had healed Mataora said to Niwareka,

'Let us now return to the Overworld. We must leave Rarohenga.'

But Niwareka just stared at him. Then she took a step back from him and said,

'No. I think I will stay here.'

She had made up her mind to remain with her people where she felt she would be protected. But Mataora begged her to go with him. Finally she agreed to ask Ue-tonga's advice. Ue-tonga was firm.

'No. Mataora, you must return to your own world. Niwareka will stay here.'

Then he looked straight into the eyes of his son-by-marriage and said,

'I have heard that in the Overworld sometimes wives are beaten by their husbands!'

Mataora reddened with shame and said nothing.

'You must go, Mataora,' continued Ue-tonga. 'Niwareka does not want to be attacked by you again.'

But Mataora would not give her up lightly. He made Ue-tonga a promise.

'I will promise you that from now on I will not be violent or lose my temper, or strike Niwareka again. I will follow the good and gentle ways of Rarohenga.'

This time Ue-tonga was convinced that his son-in-law was sincere.

'I believe you,' he said. 'I think that you will be true to your word. Take my beautiful daughter and go to your Overworld. But as it is a place of darkness, and Rarohenga is a place of unending brightness, take our light into your world!'

'Look at my face,' replied Mataora. 'You have carved the designs and the patterns of the Underworld and I will take these to my world. I promise I will take all the goodness from your Underworld – your moko, your peaceful living, and your Niwareka.'

With that, Mataora and Niwareka set off. They reached the entrance of the tunnel leading to the Overworld and found the fantail waiting.

'You will need someone to guide you,' it said, 'because I must leave you here. So take Popoia, the owl, and Peka, the bat, with you.'

Mataora replied, 'But if I take them they will be chased by all the forest animals in my world.'

'No, they will be fine. They will hide in the darkness of the night,' said the fantail.

So Mataora and Niwareka took with them Popoia and Peka to show them the way back through the tunnel, and they became birds of the night, as the fantail had said.

When they arrived at the House of the Four Winds the guardian was waiting for them.

'What is in the bundle that you carry?' he asked Niwareka.

Niwareka looked flustered. Then she said, 'Oh, it's nothing. It's only clothes to wear in the Overworld.'

The guardian frowned, because he knew that something secret was hidden in the bundle, something that should never leave Rarohenga.

'You have tried to leave with something that belongs to our Underworld and take it to the Overworld,' he said. 'Because of this, I will never allow anyone to journey again from Rarohenga to the Overworld. This way will be closed, and from now on only the spirits of the dead may pass on their way to Rarohenga. You have there the garment of Te Rangi-haupapa. Show it to me.'

'It is so,' said Niwareka, for she had brought it hoping to use it as a pattern for the cloaks of the women in the Overworld. Reluctantly she placed the bundle in the guardian's hands and he unrolled it. Its colours were radiant and, as he held it up, the cloak shone and sparkled in that gloomy place, and Niwareka was very disappointed that she could not keep it.

So, Mataora and Niwareka passed on their way to their life, and lived happily for the rest of their days. It was Mataora who handed down the techniques and artistry of the moko from the Underworld, and it was Niwareka who taught her daughters the patterns and colours used to weave beautiful skirts and ceremonial cloaks, and these skills were passed on from her daughters to their daughters.

Legends
about Lakes,
Rivers
and Trees

The Enchanted Hunting-Ground

Long ago, near a beautiful lake called Waikaremoana, there was another, much smaller lake that was enchanted. It was enclosed by tall trees which were filled with colourful birds of every kind. It was an ideal hunting-ground and although there were many bird-spearing competitions there was never any shortage of birds.

Now a certain chief who had the hunting rights to this enchanted place used to take his wife with him on his expeditions. Before they set off he always reminded her that she must never walk in front of him carrying food of any type in case the enchanted lake was offended.

For many years the chief hunted happily and successfully around the lake until one day his wife, who had become a little forgetful, suddenly walked across her husband's path carrying food. The minute she'd done it she remembered his words and hurried back to walk behind him again.

They returned home, hoping that the gods had not noticed her carelessness. But the very next time the chief set out for the lake he searched and searched but could not find it. And it has not been seen since.

The Trees of the Forest

It was a glorious sunny day, and the trees had gathered together in the forest to discuss which of them could stretch the tallest. The talk led to argument and the totara's voice could be heard clearly above all the others.

'I will be king of the forest!' it boasted. 'I will show you that I am the tallest and so you will all bow to my majesty.'

The rimu tree only laughed and said,

'Wrong! It's *I* who will be king of the forest.'

And so it went on. The rata claimed it could stretch the highest and so did the tawa.

The totara grew impatient.

'All you can do is talk,' it said. 'Watch me. I can reach our Sky Father!'

With that, there was a cracking sound as the totara stretched and stretched. But no matter how much it strained and pushed it could not reach the sky and when it realized this it let out a groan of disappointment and shame. Its groan was just like the sound a totara log makes today when it is burnt in the fire.

The forest still rang with cracking, bursting noises as the other trees also tried to reach the sky. But they too failed.

It was the totara, however, who was most ashamed as it had boasted the loudest. And so, it retreated deep into the heart of the forest where it could hide among a tangle of other trees, never to show its once-proud face again. To this day, it is surprisingly difficult to pick out the dark green outline of the totara tree from the other trees of the forest.

Lake Te Anau

 High up in the mountains in the south-west corner of the South Island is Lake Te Anau. Once, however, there was no lake here, only a long deep gully where some people from the Waitaha tribe had made their home.

In the middle of their village was a magical spring which was said to be bottomless. Only the tohunga, Te Horo, and his wife, who had been appointed guardians of the well, were allowed to go near it. This was because the people believed that if a common person looked at the water in the well, disaster would fall on the whole village. The villagers were so terrified of a possible disaster that they always diverted their gaze from anything that was close to the well, even the surrounding bushes. Te Horo used to go there and draw enough fish from it to feed the village.

One day a messenger came running into the village with bad news about a war that had broken out between certain tribes on the coast.

Te Horo, who thought that some of his friends might be involved, decided to see if he could help to make peace.

So, having consulted the people of his tribe, he set out the very next day, but not before reminding his wife not to let anyone near the spring while he was away.

The tohunga's wife was young and beautiful and a little frivolous. When she was sure that her husband had gone she called on one of the men of the village, with whom she was in love. Together they dashed into the woods, like two children on an adventure, and found themselves at the place where the magical spring stood. Then, giggling, she dared him to look into it.

'Not unless you do,' he answered.

And so they both peered in, just for a second.

That quick glance at the water was enough to break the tapu. They stood there and watched in horror as the water rose to the top of the well, spilled over and flooded the whole village.

Now Te Horo happened to look back on his long journey towards the coast and he knew that something terrible had happened. All he could see was a sheet of water. His village, his tribe, his valley, all had been drowned under a great expanse of water.

Te Horo knew, at once, that someone in the village must have betrayed his trust, and that this disaster was punishment from the gods. And he was filled with sadness because he knew that he would never see his wife, his people or his village again.

Hotu-puku

One day a small group of people from Taupo set off northwards to visit friends at Lake Rotorua. After a few days, when they had not returned home, their relatives became worried. Had they decided to stay on a little longer, or had something terrible happened to them? They waited one more day and still there was no news.

So, the chiefs of the tribe gathered in the centre of the village to discuss what they should do. Just then they spotted some figures in the distance, striding in their direction. Full of hope, they walked out to greet them. But, when they got closer they could see that these were not their missing friends but some visitors from the Rotorua region. Straightaway they asked them for news of their relatives. But the visitors had not seen them anywhere along their route.

The chiefs now feared the worst: their relatives must have been attacked and imprisoned by an unknown enemy. Gathering together warriors from all the neighbouring villages they set out across the plain, taking a different path to the one the visitors from Rotorua had used.

'No enemy is too strong for us!' they shouted as they walked.

What these brave warriors did not know, however, was that they were fast approaching the territory of the terrible taniwha Hotu-puku who had already attacked and devoured their relatives. This, then, was no ordinary enemy.

It did not take Hotu-puku long to catch the scent of human flesh. Suddenly the warriors heard an unearthly roar and saw a massive black body, bigger than the biggest whale and hideous with its covering of spines and lumps, lashing its long, thorny tail as it crashed down the mountain towards them. They fled in terror as the taniwha trampled everything in its path. Only the speediest runners escaped death: the others were seized in its razor-sharp teeth and crunched into pieces.

The few survivors struggled northwards until they reached one of the villages at Rotorua where, still in a state of shock, they tried to describe the horrors of their ordeal. The Rotorua warriors immediately armed themselves and, swearing revenge on the taniwha, marched south to the mountain where Hotu-puku had his lair. They made camp on the lower slopes and set to work, plaiting leaves into strong ropes.

At nightfall they climbed up the mountain, making sure to stay downwind of the taniwha all the time, and laid the ropes in a trap on the ground, some distance below his cave. Even in the dark they could make

out the devastation all around them: trees and bushes were snapped in two and clothes and weapons lay scattered about.

Only the youngest and bravest of the warriors were allowed to climb up to the cave itself. As they got closer they were nearly deafened by the noise of Hotu-puku's snoring. Suddenly the snoring changed to an even louder rumbling as Hotu-puku, who once more caught the scent of humans, started to move. The young warriors were terrified at the sight of this monstrous creature, with its blood-shot eyes, vicious-looking spines and deadly tail, as it lumbered out of the cave. But they stood their ground until the last moment, determined to lure him into their trap.

Hotu-puku was so greedy for another meal that he did not even notice the coils of rope further down the slope. As the warriors tore down ahead of him he opened his slavering jaws wide and ran straight into the trap. His tail and one leg were snared instantly, and as he pulled to free himself the ropes tightened. The harder he pulled, the harder the warriors heaved on the ropes. They had staked them so firmly that Hotu-puku, even with the full weight of his massive body, could not break a single one. As he thrashed about in rage, howling with pain, he was pinned down by yet more ropes.

The elders of the tribe were so angered by Hotu-puku's massacre of their friends that they had decided that even though they were old, they should be the first to strike the taniwha. So, the oldest man present pulled out his weapons and slashed the taniwha with a powerful blow, across the face and across one of his limbs. He was followed by one of the young warriors who had bravely roused the taniwha outside his cave. The rest of the warriors then surged forwards, stabbing and cutting like madmen until, at last, the taniwha crumpled, lifeless, to the ground.

At first the men walked all around his carved up body, amazed at its enormity. Then, using their sharp knives and swords made of sharks' teeth, they cut through the layers of fat and discovered, to their horror, broken limbs, axes, meres, and cloaks. They paled at this gruesome sight.

Gathering up these remains, they buried the bodies of their friends. Then, to show their contempt for Hotu-puku, they cooked part of his body and ate it. Their revenge was complete.

To this day, that taniwha's awful shape and size is talked about in the village of Taupo as its attack on their relatives was the most terrible thing that ever happened to their tribe.

Putawai

This is the story of a Maori youth called Wetenga who is caught by a wairua, a spirit, and used as bait to trap his girl Putawai.

The Maoris believe that once a mortal enters the vast underworld home of the spirits, he or she can never return. For this reason, Wetenga thought that once Putawai had been taken to the spirit world he would never see her again.

Wetenga was a young warrior. One day he and a few friends decided to go hunting in the forest to provide for the evening meal. They had arranged that if they became separated they would call to each other with a special shout. This worked well for quite a while but then Wetenga grew so concerned about catching enough birds that he wandered out of shouting distance. Without realizing it, he had suddenly lost contact with his friends.

Wetenga carried on hunting for several hours and although he knew he was alone he was not really worried as the tribe knew where he was. He was just thinking about looking for the track that led back to his village when he heard crashing noises in the distance, and loud shouting. All of a sudden a big man appeared out of the bushes and asked Wetenga who he was.

Wetenga told him who he was and what he was doing. He explained that he was trying to find his way back to his friends.

'Well,' said the stranger, 'don't worry. I'll show you the way.'

With that, he set off, in a determined way, and Wetenga felt confident that he would be all right if he followed this stranger.

For several hours they walked and walked. Gradually Wetenga began to feel that something was wrong, that he was being taken in circles

rather than a direct line. Perhaps the stranger is lost, he thought.

Having been hunting for so many hours, Wetenga became exhausted. But the stranger kept up the pace, and seemed to grow stronger and stronger. Finally, out of breath and stumbling, Wetenga tripped on the roots of a tree and fell, almost knocking himself out as he hit the ground.

The stranger just laughed and said,

'You see, you are not so strong! What a warrior!'

Then he grabbed hold of Wetenga, who was stretched out on the ground, and tied him up.

'You silly fool to trust me, Hiri-toto. I am a wairua and I am growing hungry for a good feast of young women. The women from your tribe will do nicely and you will make good bait.'

The colour drained from Wetenga's face as he realized how he had been trapped and how his own, beautiful Putawai, whom he loved so much, was in terrible danger as she would be sure to come looking for him as soon as she knew that he was missing.

Wetenga felt powerless to do anything as the evil wairua dragged him away to his cave. There he tied Wetenga to a tree with vines and left him.

When the hunters returned to their village without Wetenga Putawai came running up to them to ask where he was.

'Don't worry!' they said. 'He's hunting and he'll be with us soon. Somehow we became separated but Wetenga will find his own way back, don't you worry.'

Putawai did worry. She knew that Wetenga was sure of himself and sure of the forest but something told her that this time all was not well.

For several days she waited for him to return. One day followed another and still there was no sign of him. Putawai could take it no longer and went to the chief.

'There must be something wrong,' she said. 'It is many days now since Wetenga disappeared and he has not returned. Please, you must send out a search party, and I will accompany them. He may be hurt or even unconscious and perhaps only the sound of my voice will rouse him.'

The chief agreed and early next morning a search party of villagers, accompanied by Putawai, left for the forest. They searched and searched but with no success. They stopped to rest and Putawai went a little way off and found a stream. As she bent down to drink she heard loud

shouting. Looking up she saw the huge shadowy figure of Hiri-toto striding towards her. She was paralyzed with fear.

'Ha!' he roared, 'I've found one.'

And with that, he threw her over his shoulder and flew up above the tree tops. When he came to a valley he dropped down to where there was a deep hole in the ground. Through this he descended into the underground world of the spirits with Putawai, his mortal booty.

Putawai, who had been in a trance since she was lifted into the air, suddenly came to and was frightened by the strange unnatural light and by the crowds of pale-faced wairua who were jostling to get a better view of her. Then she recognized Hiri-toto's voice.

'What do you think of my young, beautiful plump pigeon, eh? Make sure you guard her well because you know these people are very tricky to catch. Now that I have this one she is our prize for the night! Keep a sharp eye on her while I go and see to the preparations for the ovens.'

Poor Putawai could not stop trembling. This Underworld, these wairua were terrifying and she could not think of any way of escaping from Hiri-toto's macabre feast.

Just then another wairua approached and stood close to Putawai, watching her with compassionate eyes. He had seen Hiri-toto bring

many beautiful young women into this place and kill them, and he felt very sorry for Putawai. He turned to the wairua who were guarding her and said,

'What are you waiting for? Go off and help Hiri-toto. He needs firewood and other things to prepare this feast.'

The wairua responded to his voice of authority and as they turned to go he made a sign to Putawai not to speak, indicating that she was in safe hands. So she sat still while the wairua went to help Hiri-toto. Then her rescuer whispered,

'My name is Manoa. I have no liking for what Hiri-toto does and what he is. I do not like the way we all must eat the young women he catches. We could escape. Would you come with me? I will take you safely over the trees and you will be my wife in another part of this spirit world.'

Putawai was not sure whether she would ever see the real world again but at least here was a chance of some kind of life. The wairua would be back soon to claim her for the evening feast so she had to make up her mind quickly.

'Yes,' she said, 'I will come with you.'

'Throw your arms around my neck. Hold on to me tight and we will fly through the trees.'

So they did, and they escaped and flew for a considerable distance until they alighted in the underworld home of the ngerengere who were hideously deformed.

Hiri-toto and his friends, who were hot on their heels, found them in no time at all and started to attack. The ngerengere, who were so frail and weak, could not protect the runaways so Manoa swept Putawai up again and headed, this time, for the safety of his own underworld village. Hiri-toto was furious when he discovered that Putawai was being sheltered by Manoa's tribe but there was nothing he could do about it. In disgust, he turned back. And Manoa and Putawai became husband and wife.

Several hours after Putawai's disappearance Wetenga was found by his friends. He was close to death. The vines round his wrists and ankles had cut deeply into him and he had had no food or water for many, many days.

The search party brought him back to the village and did all that they could to revive him. For weeks on end Wetenga lay there, drifting in and out of consciousness. He kept dreaming about Putawai, dreaming that something terrible had happened to her. It was only when he was fully conscious that he realized the truth: that Putawai had been taken to the Underworld, where no man could follow, to become the prized dish of the evil wairua Hiri-toto.

Gradually, Wetenga picked up the pieces of his life again and tried to bury his grief.

One day Wetenga saw a strange woman in his village. He welcomed her and asked her name. The woman answered in a soft, quiet voice,

'My name is Putawai.'

Wetenga, thinking he had misheard the name, asked her again.

Once more she answered, 'My name is Putawai.'

'I have known a Putawai,' said Wetenga.' She was promised to me in marriage. She was my love – we loved each other very much. But she has been eaten by a wairua.'

And Putawai said, 'She has not. It is me, I am here, I have come back.'

Wetenga was stunned. He tried to speak.

'But I . . . this is not . . . it's not true, you are supposed to be dead!'

'Please,' said Putawai, 'take me in your arms and hold me and you will know that I am real, that I am yours, your Putawai.'

Nervously, Wetenga stretched out his arms and folded them round her. Only then did he believe that she was his Putawai, the Putawai that he thought he had lost for ever.

Wetenga was overjoyed. Putawai had returned, returned from the wairua world – a thing that was not possible. He asked her if she would marry him without delay and she agreed. Wetenga was the happiest man in the tribe.

Putawai, however, had a secret that she brought with her from the spirit world. On her wedding night she told Wetenga about the things that had happened in the Underworld but she did not tell him the whole story.

One night Wetenga woke to the sound of a baby crying. It was the cry of a very young baby. He stretched out in the darkness and felt his wife's body and beside her that of a baby.

'What has happened? Where does this baby come from?' he asked.

And Putawai said, 'I must tell you now. For a short while in the other world I was married to a wairua, and this is his child. I cannot hide it any longer.'

Wetenga was greatly distressed at hearing this because he thought that now he had lost Putawai again, that she would go with her child to the spirit world.

'What happens to the child when the light comes?' he asked.

'Do not be afraid, husband, the child is a wairua and has no place in our world. Manoa will come just before dawn and take the child back. In the dark hours he will return the child to me.'

Now Wetenga was not happy at the idea of a wairua visiting his home every morning and night. He decided to sit up and wait for Manoa. Then he would kill him.

Wetenga waited, club in hand, but as the dawn started to break he fell asleep. Night after night, dawn after dawn, the same thing happened. Wetenga was growing more and more frustrated because he could not stay awake long enough to catch Manoa. Suddenly he realized that a wairua magic spell had to be the cause of his drowsiness just before dawn. Still, Wetenga got himself ready each night to fight Manoa, still sleep overtook him.

The weeks passed and one night Wetenga realized that he had not heard the baby cry. He stretched out his arms and felt nothing but the body of Putawai.

'Where is the child?' he asked.

'The child is ready to be weaned. Manoa has taken it to its true home where it can now live for the rest of its days.'

Wetenga felt as if a great weight had been lifted off his chest. There would be no more nightly visits from the wairua. Putawai and he could resume their lives together in peace once more.

Wetenga and Putawai grew to love each other even more and all thoughts of the wairua and of what had happened between the two of them seemed to disappear. They never again talked about the strange spirit world of the wairua.

Rona and the
Legend
of the Moon

There are many legends about heavenly bodies but there is none more popular than the story of the woman in the moon. This is about a woman called Rona who swore at the moon god. To fully understand this story you should know that swearing at a god is a shocking thing to do. Even worse, the actual word that Rona used, pokokohua, means 'cooked head' and implies something really filthy. Rona's fate has inspired the old proverb 'Kia mahara ki te he o Rona', *Remember the wrongful act of Rona.*

Rona was very much loved by her husband and her sons but, unfortunately for them all, she was very quick tempered. From time to time, and with little or no reason, she would flare up and scream and shout and become very abusive. Her husband was sad about this and though he loved her dearly, sometimes even he wanted to get away from her, to escape her lashing tongue.

One night, when the moon was full, Rona's husband announced that it was a good night for fishing and that he would go to an island, not far away, with his two sons, and they would fish and not return until the following night. 'When we do return,' he told Rona, 'it will be just at dusk and we would like you to have the meal ready.'

So Rona said goodbye to her husband and her sons and settled down to wait for their return. The following day she made preparations for the meal. She lit the fire early and placed stones on top. As the sun was going down it was time to sprinkle water on the hot stones, lay the food on top and cover it all with leaves and earth. Just then she heard, in the distance, the sound of the fishermen chanting as they made their way back home.

Suddenly she remembered that she had not fetched the water so she rushed down the path towards the spring with a gourd in each hand.

Darkness had fallen and as she ran the moon slipped behind a heavy cloud. Rona stumbled and fell, but she picked herself up and found her way to the spring where she filled up the gourds.

On the way back it was still pitch black and she fell again and the water sloshed out of the gourds. Not only had she spilt the water but she skinned her knee badly as well. The pain and the exasperation she felt were too much for her and she lost her temper. She opened her mouth and screamed abuse at the moon.

'You've withdrawn your light, how dare you! Pokokohua! Pokokohua!'

The moon was normally serene and detached, but he could not ignore such an insult. He spun down and caught Rona in his hands, intending to snatch her up into the sky. But Rona caught at a branch of a ngaio tree and held on for dear life. The moon, however, was extremely strong and as Rona clung to the tree he pulled and pulled until the roots of the tree were torn out of the ground. Then he swept Rona high up into the sky and placed her on the surface of the moon.

When Rona's husband and sons returned they found the stones still glowing and the uncooked food still lying beside the fire. But there was no sign of Rona. It was not until he looked up at the moon and saw the shape of a desolate woman holding two gourds that Rona's husband realized that she had cursed and screamed one time too many. His poor hothead of a wife would remain there, floating across the sky on the face of the full-bodied moon, for the rest of her life.

Hutu and Pare

Hutu was a young warrior. He was extremely good-looking and skilful at the art of spear- and dart-throwing.

One day there was a great gathering at one of the villages and while he was there Hutu took part in a dart-throwing competition. As the games progressed it was obvious that Hutu would be the winner. Naturally, he was pleased with his performance, but he would have been even more delighted if he had known that he was being observed by a beautiful puhi called Pare.

Being of very high rank, Pare was kept apart from the rest of the village. She was surrounded by servants who had been carefully selected to protect her.

From her house Pare watched Hutu and fell in love with this handsome young stranger. As the competition drew to a close the darts, which were shaped like slender spears, were thrown, with great accuracy, further and further away. One of Hutu's darts landed very close to Pare's house.

Pare dashed out, picked it up and ran back to her hut. Hutu saw that she had picked up his dart and went to retrieve it. He followed her, but only to the door of her house, and asked if he could please have the dart back. She told him that she would not part with it unless he came inside her house. This was, of course, a plain declaration of love in line with established custom. Hutu knew this but refused to go in: he told her he was afraid that her people would set upon him.

Pare was not at all pleased with his response. She tossed her head haughtily and said her people would do *exactly* what she told them to do. Hutu then told her the real reason for his refusal: he had a wife and two children and must protect them.

Now because Pare was so isolated from normal village life she did not know the ways of everyday relationships between people. This was the first time she had fallen in love and she could not cope with Hutu's rejection of her. Overcome with misery, she went into her house, locked herself in the central room and killed herself.

A short while after Hutu's departure Pare's attendants noticed how quiet the house had become. They went to check on their mistress and, to their horror, found that she was dead. They could see that she had killed herself. Their horror turned to terror when they realized that because they had failed in their duty to protect her, they were also in danger of losing their lives. They knew that Hutu was the last person to speak to Pare, so it would be easy to point the finger at him. They would blame him.

They ran to the chief and broke the terrible news, saying that Hutu was obviously the person who had killed her. The elders of the tribe gathered together and said that Hutu would have to be put to death.

Hutu protested his innocence, explaining that he had done the right thing by refusing to go into her house. But the elders would not change their minds. Hutu was to be put to death.

Hutu made one request.

'Could I have three days to pray to my gods and to prepare myself for death?' he asked.

The elders agreed to this postponement but ordered that Hutu be kept in isolation.

Now Hutu had remembered some of the prayers that were chanted by the priests of his tribe at the deathbed of a chief. Although he was not a priest himself, he thought that if he could repeat the most powerful of these prayers, perhaps he could make his spirit leave his body and find Pare. So, using all his powers of concentration, he started to chant, and soon his spirit did separate from his body. His body was left lifeless on the floor and his spirit lifted up and began its journey to the Underworld.

He passed the guardians of the Underworld and at last reached the place where the souls of the dead go about their daily work. He was told that Pare had gone into the house made ready for her, but that she had refused to speak to anybody there. Hutu had to find some way of making

Pare come to him, and also of getting them both safely back to the Overworld. He hit on a good plan.

First of all he gathered a group of younger spirits and told them he could show them a new game. He took them into the forest, not far away, and found a group of trees that were tall and straight. He lopped the branches off one and then tied long ropes to the top. With the help of the others, he pulled it hard so that the trunk bent over in the shape of a bow.

Next, he asked the spirits to hold on to the ropes while he and one of the spirits climbed up the trunk. When they were at the end he shouted, 'Now, let go!'

They let go of the ropes and the tree sprang back up and Hutu and his companion flew into the air. They landed safely on the ground quite some distance away.

The spirits were very excited. They laughed and shouted and gave a loud cheer as Hutu made his way back to them. The sound of all this excitement brought Pare out of her house. She watched as the young spirits all clambered to have a go at this new game. Suddenly her eyes met Hutu's, and she smiled. She walked up to him and said,

'Let me do that! I'd like to try, but please, let us do it together. Let me sit close to you and hold on to you.'

Hutu was delighted that the first part of his plan had worked. Now he could try the second. He asked even more spirits to come and give a hand with the pulling so that they could bend the tree even closer to the ground. Then he and Pare climbed up and when they had reached the top he told her to hold on tight. Then he shouted at the spirits,

'Pull hard! Down further, even closer!'

They pulled with all their might until the top of the tree touched the ground. Then Hutu shouted, 'Now!'

They dropped the ropes and the tree bounced up with such force that Pare and Hutu were thrown high into the roof of the Underworld where Hutu grabbed at the roots of a tree that was growing down from his world. Pare hung around his neck and, once they had got their breath back, they started to climb. Together they worked their way up through the soil, using the roots as footholds, until they reached the surface of the Overworld. They climbed into the sunlight, shook the soil off their bodies, and, hand in hand, walked through the forest until they reached Pare's village. There, without anyone observing them, the two souls re-entered their bodies.

Pare stood up and walked out into the village and showed herself to her people. There was great rejoicing because she had returned. Hutu was immediately released and pardoned for the 'death' of Pare, and he was allowed to return to his own tribe.

What happened then no one knows for certain. But there are those who say that Hutu eventually returned to Pare and that they had many children and that Hutu kept both wives. The gods would have been happy to see him with two wives and many children.

From then on, Hutu was known as Pare-hutu, perhaps because Hutu had given Pare the gift of a second life.

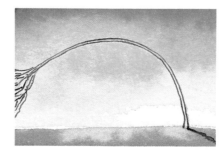

Three Little Bird Legends

The first of these legends is the story of how Kaka, the large parrot, got his very beautiful red feathers. The second tells of how Toroa, the lonely albatross came to roam the oceans. And the third, of how Maui gave the robin its snowy white cap of feathers.

The Ground Parrot and the Albatross

Kakapo and Toroa were arguing about which of them was the superior bird, worthy of becoming leader of all the birds in the land.

Kakapo said,

'Let's have a competition. Whichever of us can hide from the other without being found is the winner. Albatross, you hide here in this bare stretch of land. There are no trees, no shrubs and no bushes. You hide from me, and I will find you.'

Toroa laughed at him and said,

'Ha! *I* am the greater bird. I will be able to hide from you – there's no doubt about that – and you won't be able to find me.'

So Toroa found what he thought was a perfect hiding place, made a little dip in the earth, tucked his wings in and crouched down as low as he could. He lay there like a stone.

Now there was a strong wind blowing and although Toroa lay quite still his white feathers were being ruffled and it did not take Kakapo long to spot them. He pounced on Toroa saying,

'See! I *have* found you!'

Toroa was bitterly disappointed at being found and begged the ground parrot for one more chance.

Kakapo, being a fair bird, agreed.

Once again Toroa hid as best he could and once again his white plumage gave him away.

Then Kakapo said,

'Right. Now it's my turn.'

He scurried around until he found a natural dip in the land. As luck would have it there was some fern nearby so he covered himself with it.

When Toroa flew into the air to search for Kakapo he could not see the parrot anywhere. The fern made a perfect camouflage.

'Come out! Come out!' cried Toroa eventually. 'I can't find you.'

Kakapo, who had been keeping an eye on Toroa as he floated above, high in the sky, called out,

'I will give you one more chance.'

So he did, and once again the albatross was unable to find the ground parrot. Toroa was defeated by the camouflaged Kakapo.

It was decided that Kakapo's cunning had won him the competition and the title of leader of all the birds. Toroa the albatross, they decreed, was not fit to live on land.

And so the albatross was banished to a life spent patrolling the lonely oceans of the sea goddess Hinemoana. Kakapo, the ground parrot, can be seen happily pecking out a living among the flax that grows on the riverbanks.

Kakariki and Kaka

 Kakariki was just a little parrot covered in green feathers but when he stretched out his wings to fly, flashes of brilliant red gleamed underneath the green.

One day Kakariki was in the forest with a big, strong parrot called Kaka who had brown feathers. Kaka was fed up with his dull plumage and was envious of Kakariki's red feathers. He decided to brighten himself up. He knew that Kakariki liked him so he thought it might be quite easy to persuade the small bird to lend him some red feathers.

'Kakariki,' he said, 'you see those beautiful feathers that you have, those beautiful red feathers? Why don't you lend them to me for a little while? I would like to wear them to be as beautiful as you, but I won't keep them for very long.'

Kakariki, who was trusting and generous, thought to himself, 'Yes, I can share them with Kaka. No reason not to.'

And so he pulled out all his red feathers and gave them to Kaka to try on. But Kaka did not wait to try them on: as soon he had them safely in his claws he made off, as fast as he could go, deep into the forest.

Kakariki ran after him, calling and searching. But Kaka was already far away, prancing about in the trees admiring his shiny, new feathers.

And so it is now Kaka that owns the beautiful red feathers that flash in the sunlight when he flies, and Kakariki is simply a sad green parrot.

Maui and the Birds

When Maui was growing up at the home of Tama, the sea god, he found he had a special way with birds. In no time at all he knew all their names and habits, and they seemed to understand what he said to them.

Then, when he returned to his own family he used birds for some of his tricks. Once he changed himself into a pigeon, using the brightly coloured feathers of his mother's apron for the irridescent plumage.

Another time he was chased by his angry grandmother, Mahuika, and tried to escape by turning himself into a hawk. Later he grabbed hold of a fantail that belonged to Mahuika and squeezed it until the little bird's eyes stuck out and its tail stood up and turned slightly to one side, as it does today. The fantail got its revenge in the end for when Maui went on his last, fatal journey, accompanied by flocks of birds, it was the fantail's loud laughter that woke the Great Lady of the Night and so caused Maui's death.

One day, long before the fantail's revenge, Maui was working in the full sun and became very thirsty. He called to the saddleback bird.

'Bring me water. I am so thirsty, so hot! Will you please bring me water!'

The saddleback refused so Maui threw it into the water.

Then he asked the stitchbird, but it would not obey either. So Maui, who was beginning to get really cross, threw it into the fire and its feathers were singed.

The third time he asked the gentle robin, who had always been Maui's friend.

'I'll bring you water,' said the robin. 'It won't be very much – just a drop, but maybe that'll be enough.'

Maui thanked him and said,

'Yes, you truly are my friend.'

And, as a mark of his appreciation, Maui turned the feathers at the front of the robin's head a distinctive, snowy white.

The robin had only managed to bring a small drop of water and Maui was still thirsty. So, he called to the orange-wattled crow.

'Please bring me some water. I am so thirsty.'

The orange-wattled crow filled its ears with water and brought it to Maui. Maui rewarded it by stretching its legs until they were long and slender so that it could paddle through the water with great ease in search of food.

Glossary

kiwi	flightless bird
kokako	blue-wattled crow
moko	facial tattoo (full face in men, lips and chin in women)
ngerengere	leprosy sufferer
patupaiarehe	sprite, fairy
puhi	virgin
taniwha	spirit, monster
tapu	sacred, prohibited
tiwaiwaka	fantail
tohunga	priest, expert
wairua	spirit

ngaio	
pukatea	
rata	all New Zealand
rimu	native trees
tawa	
totara	